Rising Parent Media, LLC
 Published 2017
Printed in the United States of America

20 19 18 17 16 1 2 3 4

ISBN: 978-0-9987312-3-0

FOR GREAT RESOURCES AND INFORMATION, FOLLOW US ON OUR SOCIAL MEDIA OUTLETS:

Facebook: www.facebook.com/educateempowerkids/
Twitter: @EduEmpowerKids
Pinterest: pinterest.com/educateempower/
Instagram: Eduempowerkids

The paper used in this publication meets the minimum requirements of the American National Standard for Information Sciences—Permanence of Paper for Printed Library Materials, ANSI Z39.48-1992.

www.educateempowerkids.org

MESSAGES ABOUT ME: SYDNEY'S STORY

A GIRL'S JOURNEY TO HEALTHY BODY IMAGE

Educate and Empower Kids would like to acknowledge the following people who contributed time, talents, and energy to this publication.

STORY BY:
Dina Alexander, MS
Kyle Roberts, MA
Jenny Webb, MA
Edited By:
Maren Warner
Tina Mattsson

DESIGN AND ILLUSTRATION BY:
Jera Mehrdad

Special Thanks To:
Cliff Park, MBA
Byran Korth, Ph.D.

First, please read this book more than once to your child!

Using the simple discussions and activities found at the end of the book will make the experience more meaningful.

All of us receive hundreds, possibly thousands of messages every day from friends, family members, acquaintances, advertisements, social media, TV, and elsewhere.

Some of this information is unhealthy, useless, or harmful. To combat this barrage of messages, take time every day to uplift your child! As you help them fill their "accounts" by encouraging them, talking with them, and guiding them, they will learn to do this for themselves. They will see they have value as they are: beautiful, unique, and good individuals.

HOW are you?
GOOD and you?

We live in a great big world.
Every day we get messages
everywhere we go.

Some are direct...

Some are indirect...

This is a story about a girl and the messages she sees every day.

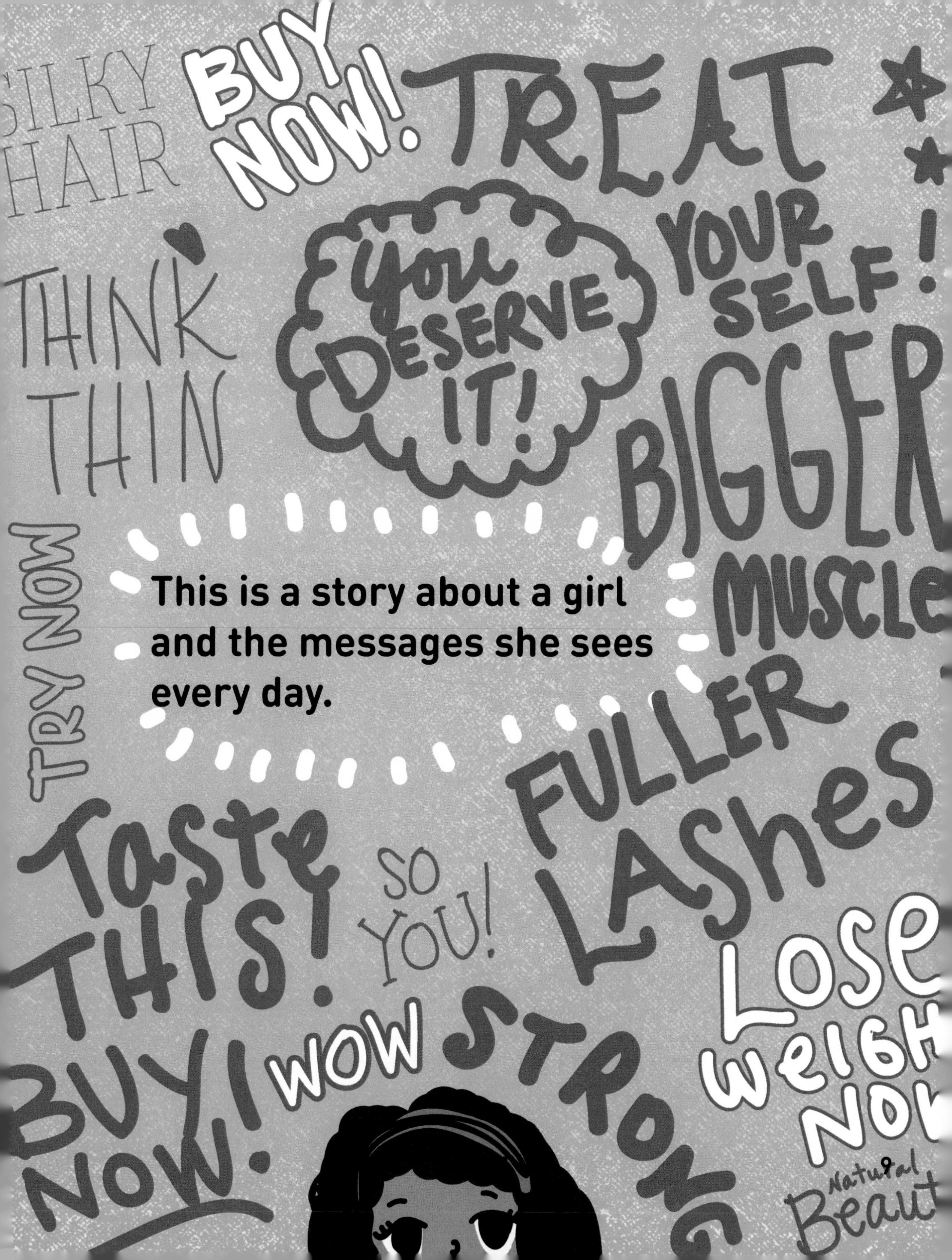

MEET SYDNEY!

She likes reading, going out for ice cream with her mom, and painting.

But most of all, she LOVES running track! Running makes her feel free and strong.

After school, Sydney likes watching TV, but some of what she sees on TV is confusing. She doesn't understand why having perfect, shiny hair makes people happy.

FOR
PERFECT, SHINY
HAIR, USE OUR
SHAMPOO.

Messages, or commercials, like this make her wonder if she is pretty enough or worry that maybe she needs to change...so she does. She doesn't understand exactly why having perfect hair seems to make people happy.

Sydney likes her own hair but thinks,

Sydney's new hair feels heavy and it takes longer to style each morning, which isn't fun at all! "How in the world will I run track with hair like this?" she wonders.

Although, she does like how shiny it is, and it makes her look more like the lady in the commercial.

Sydney posts her new hair on Instagram and notices a new lip color her friends "like" and comment about.

Big, red lips are important to her friends, so Sydney figures big, red lips must be cool.

"Having these lips makes it kind of hard to laugh, and the lipstick gets on my teeth.

And when I run track, dust sticks to the lipstick," she thinks.

BUT MY FRIENDS THINK IT LOOKS COOL!

Different advertisements pop up on the computer while Sydney works on a homework assignment. An ad to lose weight makes her wonder if she needs to lose weight.

"I run every day at practice, and the doctor says I am growing perfectly. We eat healthy at home, but I DON'T look like THAT," she thinks. "I guess I could cut out ice cream and after school snacks. Maybe that would help."

LOSE 10 LBS FAST!

So she works hard to change so she can be skinny too.

Her new diet makes her feel tired and a little grumpy. She isn't able to run as fast at practice.

ARE YOU DOING OK SYD?

Feeling worn out, Sydney decides to hang out with her friends to help herself feel better.

But even with her friends, she feels like she isn't good enough.

DID YOU SEE LAUREN'S SHOES? THEY ARE SOOOOO CUTE!
HMMMMMM, WHERE DID YOU GET YOUR SHOES?

Sydney likes her shoes. They help her run fast at track practice. And the bags that her friends carry look like a BIG hassle. But she likes these girls; they are her friends.

Sydney works harder to fit in.

Sydney is feeling off balance! It's hard trying to fit in. "Maybe a run will help me feel better," thinks Sydney, but running is difficult.

Her new shoes make her stumble. Her new bag gets in the way. Her new hair starts to droop into her eyes.

"I can't run like this," she admits sadly.

Sydney quits the track team that very day.

By the time Sydney reaches her house, her heart feels heavy. She goes into her bedroom, sits on her bed, and feels very alone. Her mind is full of doubts.

She wonders out loud,

Sydney's mom comes home and suggests they go out for ice cream. At first Sydney doesn't want to ruin her new diet, but she really wants to talk to her mom, so she agrees to go.

Mom listens as Sydney shares her feelings of doubt and confusion. "The more I try to follow what my friends are doing or what advertisements I see, the less I feel I fit in."

Mom gives Sydney an encouraging smile and says, "Messages from friends and advertising will always be there. But YOU get to decide which ones to listen to and which ones to ignore."

Mom suggests three questions that Sydney should ask herself.

- AM I HAPPY WITH THIS NEW CHANGE?

- DO I WANT THIS CHANGE BECAUSE I WANT IT OR BECAUSE SOMEONE ELSE SAYS I SHOULD?

- AM I A BETTER PERSON BECAUSE OF THIS CHANGE?

"Think about these questions. When you do, you'll know what is right for you."

The next day, Sydney realizes something about her classmate Lucy. She looks different from all the other kids.

"Why didn't I notice it before?" thinks Sydney.

Lucy doesn't make any changes to her appearance. Sydney wonders how she did that, so she decides to ask her about it.

"Lucy! I was wondering, why haven't you changed the way you look?" Sydney asks.

"What do you mean?"

"Well, you don't have the same hairdo or wear the same lipstick as everyone. You don't have the same shoes or carry around a fancy bag. Why is that? Don't you want to fit in?"

"I guess I know that I don't need to change the way I look because TV, the internet, or my friends say I should. I am happy being me, and my parents say I'm beautiful the way I am," Lucy answers.

I'M BEAUTIFUL THE WAY I AM!

Sydney thinks about her mom's questions and about what Lucy said.

"How have I changed because of what I've seen my friends doing, or what I've seen on TV or the internet?"

The more Sydney hangs out with Lucy, the more she understands she doesn't have to change how she looks or who she is for anyone. She realizes that some messages are NOT healthy and make her feel bad about herself.

Lucy's words echo in her head, "I am happy being me."

She thinks about how much she misses the way she looked and running fast.

So she decides to run.

Sydney runs as fast as she can. She runs until she can hear her heartbeat in her ears. With every stride she feels more and more like herself. She knows she doesn't have to change anything about herself to be happy.

Sydney's heart has never felt lighter. She feels like she is free to be herself. And who she is is pretty awesome.

I'M
BEAUTIFUL
THE WAY I AM!

Sometimes it is hard to remember what she learned from Lucy, but she reminds herself, "I am happy being me. I am beautiful the way I am."

Sydney runs to the track field. She apologizes to her coach and teammates and asks for a second chance. They welcome her with open arms.

"It's good to have you back, Syd," says Coach.

"Thanks, Coach, it is good to be back," replies Sydney

"No, it is good to have YOU back!" Coach shoots back with a huge smile, handing Sydney her old shoes.

Everyday Sydney still sees messages all around her. Some days it's easy to ignore them, but some days they creep in.

Whenever she feels weighed down by these messages, she remembers how free she feels when she runs.

And she will never forget how much happier she feels being herself.

PERFECTION

WORKBOOK

This is a great opportunity to talk about the messages kids and adults take in every day. Use the following questions and activities to discuss healthy body image with your child.

BODY IMAGE: How you feel about your body. Your feelings can be positive, negative or both. These feelings are influenced by individual and environmental factors.

DISCUSSION QUESTIONS

FROM THE STORY:

How did you feel when Sydney changed herself to fit the messages she saw?

What was different about Lucy?

Do you know anyone like Lucy?

How did you feel when Sydney rejected the messages from the ads?

She was really brave. Do you think you could do that?

WE SOMETIMES HEAR MESSAGES ABOUT OUR BODIES FROM PARENTS, TEACHERS, OR OTHER ADULTS AROUND US. CHANCES ARE, SYDNEY HAS OVERHEARD MESSAGES LIKE THESE:

- I'LL NEVER HAVE SKIN LIKE THAT!
- IS THAT HER NATURAL HAIR COLOR?!
- I WISH I WASN'T SO FAT!

- THAT WAS SO STUPID OF ME.
- MY NOSE IS TOO BIG.

HOW WOULD THESE MESSAGES MAKE SYDNEY FEEL?

HOW DO THEY MAKE YOU FEEL?

QUESTIONS ABOUT THE MESSAGES WE EXPERIENCE:

- What messages do you see in the world around you every day?
- Where do you feel like you see most of the messages about how your body should look or about other people's bodies?
- Why do you think TV, ads, social media, videos, and other media send these messages to you?
- What messages do your parents give you about your body?
- What messages do other family members give you about your body?
- What messages do your friends and other people give you about your body?
- Why do you think family, friends, and other people send these messages to you?
- Have you tried to change things about your body because of the messages you see?

QUESTIONS TO HELP US COMBAT UNHEALTHY MESSAGES:

- What can you do to be free from the influence of outside messages?
- What do you like about yourself?
- How do you feel when people compliment you on how you look?
- Who are the people who help you feel confident about who you are?
- What can you do if your friends speak meanly about themselves and their bodies?
- Is it a good idea to compare your body (or yourself) with others? Why or why not?

QUESTIONS TO CONSIDER WHEN YOU DO MAKE A CHANGE:

- Sometimes we want to make changes to our appearance. When you do, ask yourself:
- Am I happy with this new change?
- Does this change reflect who I am?
- Do I want to change because I want to or because someone else says I should?
- Am I a better person because of this change?

QUESTIONS TO HELP US DISCUSS HEALTHY BODY IMAGE:

- It's important to be physically healthy. How can we pursue physical health (healthy eating, exercise) without becoming obsessed?
- Nobody has a "perfect" body. How do we find the balance between trying to improve ourselves in healthy ways and accepting ourselves as we are?
- Why is being concerned about being a good person more important than worrying about the way we look?
- Is a person who is not physically fit a "bad" person? Why not?

ACTIVITY:

Everyone feels better about themselves when they hear good things about themselves. Discuss ways you and your family can compliment people without focusing on their looks.

There are hundreds of ways we can compliment others without talking about how they look.

We can compliment others for being:
kind, honest, smart, funny, brave, responsible, creative, talented, friendly, patient, hard-working, strong, thoughtful, forgiving, athletic, willing to try new things, and SO much more.

What are other ways we can compliment others without concentrating on their looks?

Practice complimenting friends, family members, and acquaintances.

Check out this article from Educate and Empower Kids for more helpful ideas on ways to compliment your child beyond their looks: http://bit.ly/1Iqrnu5

ACTIVITY:

Most people occasionally (or often) say mean things to themselves. We need to practice talking back to that mean voice. The more we practice, the better we become at speaking kindly to ourselves. When we speak nicely to ourselves, we are healthier and more successful.

Discuss times when it is hard to say kind things to yourself (when you make a mistake, get a bad grade, have an argument with someone, etc.)

> **1) Give yourself permission to say nice things to yourself, even when you have done something wrong or made a mistake.**

2) Practice saying kind things to yourself. In your mind, compliment yourself ("I am kind." "I am smart." "I make mistakes and pick myself back up." "I can help people laugh.")

ACTIVITY:

Review the following statements and decide on one or two you will pledge (promise) to do:

I promise to love my body, however I am feeling, however I look.

I pledge to say only kind things about my body.

I pledge to say only kind things about other people's bodies.

I vow to see and acknowledge my strengths and achievements.

I know I am a wonderful, unique person.

I promise to try and not compare my body to others.

I commit to not change my personality or how I act just to fit in with other people.

Reread and recommit to your pledge every time you read this book.

TIPS FOR PARENTS AND TEACHERS:

Remember, your kids are listening to you!
Stop making negative comments about your body in front of your kids!
Show your kids you love your body for what it does, not how it looks.
Teach them to speak kindly to themselves.
Avoid fashion magazines and hyper-sexualized media in your home.
Remind your kids that comparing their bodies to others is not helpful.
Focus most of your praise on what your kids do, not on their looks.
If your child struggles with their weight, help them to improve their physical health without emphasizing weight numbers and without making it a moral issue. (Your Child should NOT be shamed or made to feel like a bad person because they struggle.)

Take everyday opportunities to talk about what your kids see on TV, movies, the internet, and social media. Explain that the purpose of most media is to sell products, not accurately present real life.

Here is another simple lesson that reinforces the principals in this book:
A Simple Lesson for Teaching Your Child About Body Image
http://educateempowerkids.org/teaching-child-body-image

EDUCATEEMPOWERKIDS.ORG

If you enjoyed this book, please leave a positive review on amazon.com

For great resources and information, follow us on our social media outlets:

Facebook: www.facebook.com/educateempowerkids/
Twitter: @EduEmpowerKids
Pinterest: pinterest.com/educateempower/
Instagram: Eduempowerkids

Subscribe to our website for exclusive offers and information at:
www.educateempowerkids.org

ADDITIONAL RESOURCES

Beauty Redefined

Website: https://beautyredefined.org
Info: The Beauty Redefined mantra is: "Women are more than just bodies. See more. Be more." This expanded definition of positive body image provides the foundation for their overall mission to promote body image resilience, or the ability to become stronger *because* of the difficulties and shame women experience in their bodies, not *in spite of* those things. Through both research and personal experiences, Beauty Redefined works to arm girls and women with the tools to become resilient in the face of objectification and unreal ideals about female bodies.

4 Every Girl

Website: 4everygirl.org
For our mothers, our daughters, our sisters: Campaigning for media images that value, respect, empower, and promote the true value of every girl!

Amy Poehler's Smart Girls

Website: amysmartgirls.com/
Amy Poehler's Smart Girls organization is dedicated to helping young people cultivate their authentic selves. We emphasize intelligence and imagination over "fitting in." We celebrate curiosity over gossip. We are a place where people can truly be their weird and wonderful selves. We are funny first, and informative second, hosting the party you want to attend.

Girl Up

Website: girlup.org
Girl Up's movement is committed to empowering generations of girl leaders.

Girl Inc.

Website: girlsinc.org
Girls Inc. inspires all girls to be strong, smart, and bold through direct service and advocacy. Our comprehensive approach to whole girl development equips girls to navigate gender, economic, and social barriers and grow up healthy, educated, and independent.

Citations:

Barragan, B. (2016, November 28). Helping Kids Develop a Healthy Body Image. Retrieved March 28, 2017, from http://educateempowerkids.org/helping-kids-develop-healthy-body-image

Grossman-Scott, A. (2016, November 28). Encouraging A Healthy Body Image. Retrieved April 4, 2017, from http://educateempowerkids.org/what-healthy-body-image/

Grossman-Scott, A. (2016, December 05). When Parents Struggle with Body Image. Retrieved April 4, 2017, from http://educateempowerkids.org/parents-struggle-with-body-image/

How to raise a girl with a positive body image. (2015, June 10). Retrieved March 22, 2017, from http://www.lazymomsblog.com/2015/04/20/how-to-raise-a-girl-with-a-positive-body-image/

Male vs. Female Body Image. (n.d.). Retrieved April 12, 2017, from https://www.bradley.edu/sites/bodyproject/male-body-image-m-vs-f/

Mustard, J. (2016, April 14). The Body Image Pledge. Retrieved April 7, 2017, from http://jennymustard.com/column-the-body-image-pledge-2/

What is body image? (n.d.). Retrieved May 10, 2017, from http://www.nedc.com.au/body-image